The Ohio State University Press/*The Journal* Award in Poetry

Also by Talvikki Ansel

My Shining Archipelago
Jetty & Other Poems

SOMEWHERE IN SPACE

Talvikki Ansel

The Ohio State University Press

Columbus

Library of Congress Cataloging-in-Publication Data
Ansel, Talvikki, 1962– author.
  Somewhere in space / Talvikki Ansel.
     pages cm
  Includes bibliographical references.
  "Winner of the 2014 Ohio State University Press/The journal award in poetry"
  ISBN 978-0-8142-5224-6 (pbk. : alk. paper) — ISBN 0-8142-5224-9 (pbk. : alk. paper)
  1. American poetry—21st century. I. Title.
  PS3551.N69S66 2015
  811'.54—dc23

                              2015027795

Cover design by Regina Starace
Text design by Juliet Williams
Type set in Adobe Janson
Cover image: Ingebjorg L. Smith, Winter Snowdrop Woodcock, 2014, reprinted with
permission of the artist

9 8 7 6 5 4 3 2 1

for Joel Plessala

CONTENTS

ACKNOWLEDGMENTS

Grateful acknowledgment is made to the editors of the following journals in which these poems appeared (some in different forms):

Arts & Academe online, *The Chronicle of Higher Education*, "Glaze"

Balancing the Tides, "Their First Houses Were Bark-Roofed Caves"

Barrow Street, "Forest"

Blackbird: an online journal of literature and the arts, "Baking Soda Trading Cards: Bird Series" (as "The Bird Cards"), "Somewhere in Space"

The Cincinnati Review, "Coil / Foil / Ribbon / Loft"

Colorado Review, "If the Vulture Chooses You," "Leap Years"

The Grove Review, "Unsettled Weather"

The Kenyon Review, "How It Sounds"

Orion, "Seed Savers"

Poetry, "Calendar," "Courtship," "Mycorrhizae," "Valentine's," "Visitors," "Xylem," "Don't Tell Me"

Poetry Northwest, "The Garden Whisperer," "Jealousy, Enkidu," "Places to Swim"

Pool, "Loft," "Outpost"

The Yale Review, "Apples"

"Mycorrhizae" was published in *Poetry Daily Essentials 2007*. "Mycorrhizae," "Xylem," and "After the Party" appeared in the *Alhambra Poetry Calendar* 2008, 2009, & 2013, respectively. "Glaze" is included in *The Hide and Seek Muse*, (Drunken Boat, 2013).

The author is grateful for the support of the Lannan Foundation for a writing residency, and the Money for Women / Barbara Deming Memorial Fund. Sincere gratitude to the poet Kathy Fagan for selecting this manuscript, and to the dedicated staff at The Ohio State University Press.

LEAP YEARS

The hippo of patience
but not complacency
stares out over the frozen
landscape, icicles on the willow,
sharp sun.
Body of teak, flank grained
horizontally,
I was a tree but now
am a palm-sized hippo
in a country of snow.
Arrows in my blood,
my ancestors
became garden furniture,
a table someone places
a wet glass on
to contemplate walnuts,
silver nutcrackers in hand
like the crocodile's jaw.
My descendants
(there were flowers, there were
seeds) will become
the decks of a boat
exposed to sun
and molecules of light,
will travel to secluded coves,
night, planets, the milky way.
Will feel the planer's touch,
heels of the caulker
as he tightens the planks,
bare soles
as someone paces
and figures displacement
of the hull,
how much
fills this space, how much
empties a hollow
punched into the sea.
Leap years (or not) the days
run away from me.

MYCORRHIZAE

When you dig up a tree,
keep some soil around the roots,
webby strands
wrap the taproot, the calm anchor, reach
horizontal through duff and toad dung,
damp mould. Things move so
discreetly sometimes,
I didn't even notice.
A tiger's ear flares in shade.
Was that the water molecule's
elemental split? The sleight of hand
described on page twenty? No, not exactly,
you prop a shingle barrier up
to shelter a wind-torn cabbage sprout.
Strawberries edge the bed, an upside down
pot keeps rain from the post hole,
another adage proved: plant
at the new moon,
a stitch in time saves nine,
if you must leave, don't
go bare, take some dirt with you.

HOW IT SOUNDS

What did she hear who first lived
at the P. O.—crows, the gray-white shorebird's
piercing loud, obvious whistles,
song versus call—
          They have their own
vocabulary: chirr, chirrup, chuck and twitter
a multitude of avian mutterings.

Clatter of kerosene tins, afternoon fog
blowing in—fog horn, door slam,
letters dropped on the counter for sorting,
clang of metal swing door on the mail slot,
mallet's crack, lunge and splash

cries of terns over the salt flats.
Bird Sounds and Their Meanings,
audiograms for each song and call,
inked brush marks and loops on a graph.
The first sounds our ancestors heard,

clambering up the rock cliff, would we
recognize the Bulwers' croon,
eider's groan and mutter, wind-shift
in the spruce boughs
and depths to sound?
              It was to be an essay—
sound in the blood—*by chance,*
by love, by fate,
          query threaded through.

Our heads bent to four cups
of glistening cranberries for freezing, we hear
whistles, bird cries suited to the shrubbery,
waves of high-pitched sounds are shorter
than low and more easily blocked,
          ground dwellers'
harsh calls, low mass of the fog horn
and surf, the oars'

chunk, chunk, squeak and splash
unless you feather them,
               blades lifting
from the trees' reflections.

Audubon said turkey vultures couldn't
detect smells, yet they tore apart
his painting of a sheep carcass,
               On bright winter days
white-throated sparrows on their wintering grounds
often sing. How light affects us,
the longer days, a walk out early
by the cranberry bogs,
               "craneberries" once,
delicate pistils
angled down like a crane's bill. We're
under the sign of the heron squawk here,
though you were born under the crane's path,
bird of heaven folding its shape
down to the slough.
               I went there once
before I knew you,
or much music, though had chanced to see once
over November-red bogs
a hawk drop down on a sparrow, just that.

VISITORS

Flames from the burn barrel
flicker orange against a stormy sky,
poppies' tenacious, red petals
tissue-thin
in the path of rubble and salt wind
a seaside garden someone's tended,
bricks scrounged for a border
a whistle away from the lighthouse keeper's
field of promising tulips.
Flats and pots carried from train
to boat, onto the dock
silvered and littered with broken shells.

Belly down on the dock we watch
that other world: eel grass
lulls and sweeps in the water, speckled
with minute mussels, barnacles
small as the white spots flecking
an inflamed throat, an empty shell
rolls down a rock, unprovoked. On the radio
the shorter tennis player battles it out
and wins; we've gotten taller,
the announcer says. Iodine-tinctured,
sea-lettuce waves, undulates,
betrays currents
like wind through a harbor town,
flapping bed sheets on a line, in the square
women in headscarves gather under cover
of dusk to talk,
they have their routines—
but that wasn't to be my emphasis, at all
the garden above, and below water,

only so much after leaving
one can claim, this panoramic of poppies
another summer's summer's day. You reach
your hand down into clear water, minnows
flee the slightest vibrations.

THEIR FIRST HOUSES WERE BARK-ROOFED CAVES

dug into hillsides against sturdy trees
each person in their circle
of industry where to catch rabbits
how much meal is left does it have
mealy bugs no solitude
except those few who drifted off
from the stockade on their own
and daily prayer. Not channeling
not fiction *it grips the imagination,*
snow steady all afternoon accumulating
on the windows, I read and doze,
wake to snow on bushes, car roofs, the road
and plot where the garlic is planted,
you'd never know, cars take the road
to town slowly, that mound—the goat's
summer lean-to, beehives,
two birds grip the feeder, a hawk
in the high trees possible
they grip the feeder tightly, think
walking off like that, the last
good ship to England embarked.

OUTPOST

Wind and more wind
a thousand animals shake the brown grass
and tangle of pods
turn the field's edge inside out
sumac's scrawl
I owe so many letters
but there was less to say
beyond the bridge lights to the city
cold cracking
the *Chamaecyparis* trunks

people walked out to cast into surf
beyond the lighthouse keeper's
abandoned house
cold cement stairs
fishing was good today
fish swam in,
swam in the concentrated green
of the waves' press
someone held a baby tight
rabbit fur muff
crocheted string connecting mittens
you will not lose this mitten.

QUAIL

Quail's instinctual dash
through wet grass, rain puddles
bobcat, fowling piece.

Limp bird
pillowed on scalloped feathers, puff
cream to chestnut to horse-flank
brown, helmeted

on a bed of leeks, browning.
I, deadly element

sack's leather straps
criss-cross the chest,
three dropped onto the plain table

handsmell of plucked bird
reached to face,

wishbone too fine to want to try.

COURTSHIP

for Hudson T. Ansel

My new job is to keep the dog
entertained, this is o.k.—snow tunnels,
balls, wood to chew, extracting items—
pillows, socks, hats, pencils,
good-smelling bread knife,
I forget to feed the fire and it dwindles,
forget to turn on the front porch light,
it remains dark on the stoop.
In the Great Grandmother's country
stolen things are retrieved, they say
the dog comes back for its bone,
the ship its timber—jaggedy, dark around
bolt holes, rotted, but now dry as kindling.
The door for its hinges. But then
the cow and tree? It's a puzzle.
Down the lane, ghosts dip
from alder branches—the girls were here,
they restored the ghosts, twisted plastic bags
into heads and tattered skirts
to hang from branches, black penned faces
rise and sway in the wind,
up the lane into a different world,
where I walked from my desk and fire,
we can try—to look more closely into a wave
and see the darter there,
court the gusts behind snow.

XYLEM

The rippled world appears through icicles
wavery, thick: house, woods, cut tree,
stained glass kingdom of cells,
islands touching
edge to edge, the membrane enclosed
palisades, sloughed-off root cap.
Carry water, carry water.
Particulars rock
just inside the breakwater
like conjured-up skiffs,
imagining the world
without you, thick circle of this—
the dry cells' outward progression,
after swimming to the ruins and back,
no one to tell the news to.
Salt water suspension,
sea's nutrients coursing
round legs, arms and trunk.

DANGEROUS CAPTAIN

Curried the favor of the rich,
the mares' tails of the sky,
coiled the hawser, ignored the gale.
Yes, his glare at the helm,
haphazard reckoning. Blue seeds
of the walking bush sewn into our pockets,
couldn't evade him. Our hair tied back
we steered, hauled, looked ahead.
Some saw channel markers, or didn't,
sideways skip of a flock of petrels
behind a wave, or that wave
became which wave.

This is where the women disembarked,
and the boy with the drum, up
the pilings by the lobster pound's
stink of bait bins. Did not come back
with the milk and mail, stepped through
the rockweed-y shell shards. The wind
came up, the wind beyond the cliff-bound
houses, their flags straight out
in the storm, rock island annexed,

their own rock island of rising wood smoke
and the white gull's cry.
The dangerous captain let go,
dangerous captain they lost touch with,
they heard he left another harbor,
heard he scorned their slow selves
weeding the larkspur, sliding their identical
children into the tide pool's cradle,
counting boat shells and cockles.

THE SHIPS

A cat sleeps in the wooden box
for the instrument panel, the gauges'
silver arms and flexible wires
are elsewhere, on a workbench, their cogs
and faces soaked in calming oil.

The ships' names were *Zephyr* and *Florida*
and something else, there were four,
one disappeared, or was given away,
or appeared in a blurry photo
in another country's colors.
What are your colors? Magenta
was one, a baggy sweater, and lining
for a shirt collar. Someone used to drape
a bored cat over their neck, à la
home from the hunt.

The cat eyes the grape arbor from the box
empty of its instruments.
Magenta is a dark whirr of color,
a tunnel into a heart to crawl into
where peonies grow,
and what we once saw and said,
is like that gull landing for fish scraps,
wings and half its body
out of the port's frame and screen.

IMPOSSIBLE HERDS:

dormice, snails
peacocks and fish,
though mentioned under
pastoralism, Roman
in my Dictionary of Antiquity:
Dog of unbroken white
better to guard your sheep
and not mistaken for wolf.
For a watchdog: sharp-eared,
wolf-like by day,
not so easily seen at night.
Broken with tan agreeable
for fraternity,
O, come into my circle of fire,
alert and furred one
therewith to share
bird flesh and the ordinary barley.

IN CAPTIVITY

said the mother, they taught
each other things, how to
build a boat, the two brothers
who remembered cedar and oak
stickered up in the back yard
to dry, stacked with wood spacers
their mother was so happy to have
later for kindling, collecting the sticks
from the patches of killed grass.

One taught the others how to grow
garlic, too quickly,
so moved on to fruit, and grafting.
Apples, peaches, the trick of clover
and chives circling the trunks,
bags of human hair to ward off deer.
Espaliered pears, quince, until each
could imagine saying, years hence,
yes, funny how I learned to graft.

They cut and mixed a crust
for pecan pie, a hunter's stew,
which proved to be too much
for even the most stalwart.
Portuguese soups, elementary words
in Ancient Greek: water, scales, spicy rum.
One, with his palm against the wall
taught the intricacies of meter, tempo,
4/4, cut time, duple, 3/4.

Another taught them to sail,
his left arm the boom and mainsail,
his right took the direction of the wind,
close-hauled, wing and wing,
how to tack and jibe. Wind
from the north wall, wind from the south,
blown from a pallet in the corner,

they maneuvered around rocks, channels,
shallow bays and rivers,
practiced man overboard. Swept
into a narrow harbor in a light wind.
It took days and days. So much to learn,
by the end they knew how to approach
a dock, how to pull up, effortlessly,
to a distant mooring.

UNSETTLED WEATHER

Late summer like a hammock
suspended in a swirl of high tree branches
insects grinding away
occasional "shick" of a flicker, robins teeter
     and flap in the high cherry

rain, rain, days of rain and wind,
                  cracking, I ran
glad not to be under
that branch, locust limbs falling

leaves tossed, turning yellow, wet.
    Tomatoes,
    some still reddening
    in the days of rain, pumpkin and squash
picked, but needing a week of sun

to thicken their skins
    then straight procession down
held in a crate in the cellar,
      swan's egg turnip, a pale shoulder

parsnips packed in sand, carrots,
biennials replanted in spring
           covered in muslin
to not cross with the loose
Queen Anne's lace frothing the hill.

FOREST

Because of the pheasant
(the gift of) and recipe book open to that page
the junipers planted in the graveyard across the bridge
and rice. No, because of the egg,
pheasant hen laying a fertile clutch
the cock's cheek patch a crinkly
red coin. Or, first the field—
hedgerows with sumac and brambles
hiding place for the pheasant hen's nest
grains and ripe berries eaten for generations
pheasant brought to this field,
no, closer again: because of the pheasant,
a gift, juniper berries picked
and the cookbook, we had the new recipe to try
and company, my mother to help strip
the bones clean, mind the shot,
because of: the story of the Great Grandparents.
Outside, the pines swayed and lurched
in the cold, a mast year—bags and bags
of pinecones to start the stove
the pines swayed
the story entered the room, hovered above the beeswax flame:
the Great Grandmother came across the border
from St. Petersburg, Russia, with the girls, a visit,
and because the border was closed couldn't go back,
detail engulfing their lives,
the story hovered, the Great Grandmother's
portrait floated into the room: in sepia,
hair pulled back, hairpins, wool coat-like dress,
with the grandchildren years later
on the steps of the rented house.
One sister stayed behind in Russia
because of the house and accounts to look after,
was murdered ("Are There Bolsheviks
In Your Washroom?"—I remember a vintage poster
in a friend's bathroom). The Great Grandfather
was rowed across the river
under cover of night,
away from the home, and foundry, schoolhouse they knew,

to join the family,
except for the sister who stayed behind
because of the house and accounts,
and another sister in the forests somewhere
travelling with her husband, a forester,
disappeared, her story,
no portrait, no stairs
pine branches snapping in cold.

SWALLOWS

Summer's over and we never even drank
at the Ocean House, yellow elegance
they'll tear down. Wind sweeps the locust
leaves across fields. In the journals
of Dorothy Wordsworth: lucid days,
walks, wet skirts twisted around ankles,
scrambles up rocks and through damp moors,
swallows nest above the cottage window,
she bakes bread, cuts and turns sheets,
papers a room. Dinner in bed for her brother
William, mutton. John, the other,
captain of a great ship bound for China.
Lowering clouds and a swallow blown sideways,
comfrey and laudanum sleep, torn sheets,
an off-shore storm knocks windows.
                                    Windfalls—
hard green knobs gather wasps in the orchard.
Half-rotted, wormy, the ones we found here,
boiled and boiled to a pale jelly, celandine
or someone's hesitant birthstone,
sweet talisman against rot.

TWO GOURDS

Blue mountains in the distance,
the gourds I filched from the roadside
this morning—
round on their shadows, elliptical reachings
down from smooth spheres
on the polished tabletop,
each one a perfect cupped handsize.
Out along the fences
their trowel-shaped leaves and angled
yellow flowers grow.
Beyond, dry fields and two types
of rabbit scurry through dust—
the long-eared jackrabbit
licking a back paw,
cottontail, quick as a bowling ball
along the edge of the brush.

No seeds rattle
when I shake the fruits, scrambled strands
dry and fibrous inside,
how do they germinate?
Tissue, skin, we're made of fibres,
muscle and blood.
I brought them in to roll on the floor,
shellac to a honey sheen
and place in a bowl,
round and balanced
as phrases, words
we want to steal, remember
completely, blossom end,
stem end's porous break-off point.

A belief "in the night in which the corn grows"—
Traveler at occasional odds with the world,
did that serve you well?
Faint lines, light stippling
and clouding, freckles,
a continent of brown.

Our huge gourds at home
spread over the fence, into
the rain-soaked field
where the stunted corn grew,
long stalks twisting this way and that,
white flower beacons
for pollinators, for the skunk
scuffling among egg shells
in the mulch.
Mottled, dried, so light
they lift up into one's hands,
like blimps, just out of sight,

moon and big dipper
above the traveler's boat.
We beg someone to paint them,
carve them
into birdhouses, jugs,
instruments, stringed.
They reside
over the desk and stove,
heads knocking
in the window's loose draft.

Card 8: Baltimore Oriole

"an exotically beautiful bird with an equally beautiful song"

Hanging out laundry in spring, new song:
oriole back in the willow above the pond,
flash of orange, nest swaying below branch tips
through wind and rain, tenuous comet-shape
of grass and twine and webs.

Cards with the painted birds, miniature
portraits from baking soda boxes:
Arm & Hammer, or Cow Brand, boxes of snow.
The cards' edges stained, bent, stored in an envelope.
Put the black duck by the loon, by the scarlet tanager,
Baking Soda for all your earthly needs
familiar, white, creaky as snow.

*"for a safe fire extinguisher simply tear open
a one pound box & pour on flames"*

Card 4: Ruby-throated Hummingbird

"the two white eggs no larger than peas"

Flame red throat like a down-scalloped thumb,
this way—gray-green. That way—red,
hummingbird among orange jewelweed
and back to the spot where the feeder hung
last year. Childhood, the tabby cat
under the clothesline spotting birds
in the apple tree, bug-sized
they tear past the nicotiana's white trumpets.
One flattened on the road like a cicada but a wing up
flag in the sky—I was here, valiant for a season
scrappy among the pines, leaving behind
a lichen-covered nest, thistle-lined
on an arching branch, coconut green
Easter confection.

"soak combs and brushes in a solution of warm baking soda"

Card 19: Gull

"glassware, goblets, cut glass and crystal
sparkle when cleaned with a paste of baking soda"

Up from the harbor onto the deserted golf course
we'd sneak around the perimeter's rocks
to see the exotic pheasants on the field edge,
tangle of rockweed and mussels, oyster catchers' calls
in fog along the green. Gull carcasses
strung from bamboo poles as warnings, eye sockets
eaten out, a webbed foot folded dry. At night
rocking, rocking under constellations, Cygnus
the swan, waves lapping the boat's hull,
Card Nineteen, the gull, edges torn:

"droppin
rocks. He
thrice before,
time dropping the
height. A remark
wisdom
FOR THE GOOD
DO NOT DESTRO"

Card 7: Merganser

"the appearance . . . of a large rakish-looking duck"

In the big family
the mother drops the baby into the sister's bed, warm bottle
sweetened with baking soda, quick off
in her robe to fix breakfast. Snow falling
erased against white ice, white again
as it drops into ashen-colored water.
Mergansers dive beyond the dock, shake drops
from red, serrated bills. Past the boatyard
and cracked pavement scattered with broken clam shells,
pink flesh hinging, white curves and purple smudge.
The foundry where out back you could read your fortune
in drips on the sand: a cloud, a wing, an eighth
note slanted.

". . . a package in your medicine cabinet and on your pantry shelf"

Card 20: Mute Swan

"oarsman. The swan's
the music of a tin fish-horn
burst of melody is the creation
original nature-fakirs the poets"

"And no birds sang," wrote the scientist, fragile
egg shells cracking under the feathered weight.
The town no longer there like it was of course,
put the curlew by the mute swan by the blue-winged teal.
Carmina Burana on the record player,
hairy devils and flames dance on the cover, a swan on a spit,
the mother reads, book propped up on a jar of Sanka.
In a curled-down sleeping bag nest her toddler sleeps,
one could walk home from school for forgotten books,
elm roots buckling the sidewalk,
a tortoise shell cat asleep on a stump
behind the wisteria and white, interlacing trellis,
mushroom anchor—weight clicking the gate shut.

"for that old fashioned flavor, and tender velvety,
moist texture in butter-type cakes, use Baking Soda the new way"

Card 3: Crested Flycatcher

"for one characteristic it is well known, its habit of placing the cast-off snake skin in the lining of its nest"

Up in the martin house the great crested flycatcher
appropriated, the nestlings nestle into the cellophane
crinkly sound of a snake skin cast off
by the black snake that inches into the garden's sun.

Someone hanging out laundry,
lighting a pipe, hears that bold announcement
from the foliage. A mixed flock,
some make no nest, some nest in dark hollows, some *"friend to man
eat countless insects."* Some impale their prey: toads and mice,
insects on thorny trees, some
                              *(A remark
                              wisdom*
whistle before daybreak.

* * * *

SEED SAVERS

Impossible to catalogue them all
because half are gone
the numbers of beans, speckled and mottled,
or how they've been carried, sacks
bags and barrels, more
numerous than earthstars,
the stone called "sheep's nose,"
you lift them in your sleep. Scrounged
from grocery store's split bags, slipped
between glass and damp
construction paper to watch them grow,
Jacob's Cattle, Calypso, Pinto
against bright paper
send down their one question.

COIL / FOIL / RIBBON / LOFT

Imprint of a loop left in the close-cropped thyme,
garter snake, eastern, a ribbon snake
drops from branches overhanging
the river. The river a ribbon—it silvers
beneath the bridge and past the cow pasture
where they wade ankle deep, stick-in-the-mud
hot summer days. Shapes and unfurlings,
it must have given them pleasure
to study the heart, a pump's angles and volumes
where it was needed, to not lose sight.

Graphite marks and lofting lines, diagonals,
a grid drawn out on the white floor.
Loft a man-shape, curled, tucked, then into a dive,
lines of a woman curved on her side, elm tree limbs
and its years' circles, loft a dog, a whale,
the world of shapes drawn out against lines
on hands and knees, stepping back to look.
Sail, wing, the foil shape the wind goes under
and over—or does the foil pass through
water and wind, quick run of molecules above
and under, air rushing, lifting the wing.

released beyond this river. Its rock
namesake surfaces at low tide,
grounded.
Watch the terrible objects:
stags' horn knives, bone stays
to squeeze the ribs, moth-wing
collage—somebody stopped that,
not me.
      A train to the city,
silent shuttling of back stoops,
laundry lines. Brown woods
and tree trunks' repeating shadows,
crossing gate
man and dog
LUMBER YARD, FOUNDRY, it's only
the next town, but everyone's a stranger,
bell peal
and this gift: iridescent
chest, huge, lordly flapping—turkeys
over the adjacent tracks.

LOFT

In truth they hated it in the smoky,
crowded loft, the two sisters. Their snoring
brothers, cornered father, mother swollen
and tired, due for another birthing.
One's arms always smelling like a smoked fish,
Sarah tarried in the kitchen garden,
told the snoozing dog her litany of woes:
water to carry, a cold, pearl-buttoned
boots on a traveler. Cass culled worn-toed
socks that needed to be mended, intoned
"beautiful, beautiful" two stubborn hours,

drank water, picked meadow rue,
set in the staircase window the blue chipped cup
so that for once, stupefied, they'd see
flowers, the herb of grace, when they looked up.

PLACES TO SWIM

Summer's ambitious project—the beach and its
dark striped rocks,
stone-lined pool at the swim club,
passage where the tide flowed out behind dunes,
                    left fingers and lips blue,
tea-colored pond of black sticks where kids
            jumped off branches of an over-hanging tree,
aqua
    of indoor pool lanes,
            the white lines' circling, breaking pattern
interrupted by arms, churns and kicks.

                    *

Yellow leaves drift down—
        fish-shaped ovals, flecking slick streets,
light October rain,
almost like swimming, the walk
                through wet, late afternoon air.
In town this week, two people found goldfish
                balanced in paper cups
                        in their mailboxes.

Teal blue wool, ten rows
        to notice the wave reappear
                in the cable I'm knitting,
dusk pattern,
        you bent
                over the piano in the kitchen
picking out the lost bars of Satie
                (what could sound better?).
                Music book left
somewhere—an attic
                or with cousins by the lake.

IF THE VULTURE CHOOSES YOU

it is the deep trees of your yard,
shade of its wings over the hot square
& bare hill (moss too dry—rain
to fill it, like sponges, anemone tentacles)
studded with oaks that hide
the carcass you smell but cannot find,
a deer whisking ears at a door slam,
fox coming from the campsite, body floating,
marionette, shadowy over the path
into leafy distraction & wild azalea stamens.
You are just the creatures in the blue house
beyond the town landing, spidery figures
poking arms at the laundry line where colors
flutter. A man in S. Carolina
pulls dried grasses over a carcass hidden
to test the vultures' sight and smell.
Beyond the house, the hill is gone
rock ledge in a million million pieces
down a metal belt shaped like a chick-waterer,
a blankness, a cavern the vulture flies over,
where once was, it moves on
where once was a ridge, wing-tip turbulence
it splays each primary, each stroking air.

JEALOUSY, ENKIDU

surged through me, I wanted half
to be the one who lay
with him in the gold grass swaying
the sunburned body
murmured over, she who came down
through the plains with Gilgamesh,
saw him rise slim-hipped from the watering hole
drinking with the gazelles,
wanting the gaze that took him in,
or shaped him, slip of mud under fingers,
afternoon through the fields, old pond
mud, dragonflies on the bank,
half wanting him to be my discovery,
to put him onto the cool page's surface,
to put hands over him, the idea
of him like a cricket hopping
under the hive of clasped fingers,
no, to have him stay
at the watering hole
framed by the tall grasses, gazelles, reaching
into the distance, caught rippling
between the reflection and the drying.

HISTORY OF PRIVATE LIFE
(Pagan Rome to Byzantium)

From November to May
they didn't travel, it took a half year
to get notice of an event. A baby
was born, damn the inheritance
diluted again, your earthenware ewer
and city plan on a marble slab. Wait
the letter boat, fresh berries and milk.
Extra babies put out, exposed, for recycling
or not, those no-nonsense days. The Roman frieze
of a couple making love, and here's the servant
bringing a pitcher of water
                        & where does that take us
in this robust field: buttercups,
egg-yolk-yellow nape of the bobolink.
Wind unceasing from the river, the aspen
saplings lean, leaves blown to small buttons
all withstanding the force, shirts blown
up bared backs and columbine heads
tormented. I miss you though they doubted it,
it took so long from writing to the unfolding.

SINBAD & SKYLARK

Its first adventure was to Harbor Island
and it came home
its next adventure was to Labrador,
before it came home,
whales of the deep breached around its
heavy planks, cormorants brought fish
to its rails.

*

Tunes from the ice rink across the river, two boys test the ice under the docks,
slide from piling to piling, venture out to the scarred center, drop rocks on
the surface. On the other bank skaters circle, confetti-bright, Pavane for a
Dead Princess, Babylon, a thousand and one nights, a mockingbird teeters
on a frozen sumac stalk, scroll of gray against brown. The boat under its
white tarp and Christmas lights.

Not right, someone said, who watched, hurricane season, hatches blown
off, sails tattered and billowing in the green chop. Mud sifted into every
cushion and seam.

We made up a story: a man came home from the war and built a boat, we
found an address, scrunched-together backyards, his after-work project. Let
them go: the possible descendants we could call forever from the phone
book. This is how long it takes to put something right, the twenty-nine
pieces fitted and shaped each side of the cabin, numerous bungs, etceteras.

In summer, the rink becomes a volleyball court. Grackles, those privateers
of iridescence, fly over the river, drop their nestlings' feces into the dark
surface, to not be traced. Someone along the way replaced planks, keel
bolts, someone noted how well it was made. The mockingbird alert on the
sumac, nest squeezed into a tangle of crab-apple. A boat sinks and is passed
along, like a song.

Mud-laden sails spread out in the snow, garden to shed, across the path to the wood pile, over the tracks of birds and cats. Gray silt scrubbed off. Buckets of water, brushes, the curious dog's footprints, snow becoming a muddy swale under knees. The sails stretched between tall pines to dry, trunk to trunk against the sky, the white sails' edges ascending, catching the wind.

HERE'S THE SEA

and Uncle Bob, he's played hooky again
from the store, a brown coat down the beach
by the osprey nesting platform
two-legged figure,
his yellow Labrador up ahead. Nearer now
cigar in teeth, "a bonus day," he says and onwards.
The Lab runs ahead and back.
Last week a frozen rim
to the parking lot, crystalled dock pilings,
after days of wind a new sand chute's
blown between the dunes: a jar lid,
the *Rosa rugosa* half-buried in sand.
Rogue wave the adults imagine
the spit taken in one crash,
think how swimmers are carried out;
waves still warm and in full drag
at their feet, the kids shriek
over treasures: fish heads with white
bloated tongues. A half mile down the beach,
pilings exposed and rusted spikes
where they never imagined there'd been a dock.
Three strange jelly fish, tentacle-less,
yellow scud of foam across the sand.
Uncle Bob takes the bayside,
iridescent mussel shells spilling water,
a dead gull, forehead tucked under
bill barely visible like a yellow pencil.
Someone's moved onto the blue houseboat, started
a smoky fire in the stove. High tide
swells the basin, up to the tattered parking lots of town
Uncle Bob trundles toward
his Labrador testing the water.
Wind-blown horseshoe crabs, their gill books'
mica-thin layers so fragile
they're half the time crushed or lost
before somebody turns their complicated shells.

VALENTINE'S

Slippage time, sky darker
than yesterday,
cold snap forecasted,
a gray screen over the river
and the old fort, ice chunks.

Compost dumped, dishes washed
in two bowlfuls of water,
antifreeze poured down the drains
for night is coming.

In a Wildflower and Shrub
Guide, I identified that weird
seed pod I took a snapshot of
in sunny autumn woods.
Magenta capsule, four orange seeds
dangling on threads,
"hearts-a-bustin' with love" it's called.

From the passenger's side
I watch a gull, wing flap like a towel
drop clams from a great height
onto the icy road.

AFTER THE PARTY

The tree sparkled
in the window of the twine factory, smell
of pine tar, soap, a girl named Melissa
lived here when the street
was longer, more sand-pocked,
1797
The Art of Cookery Made Plain and Easy,
pigeons transmogrified, trying
to catch that vision on paper
or wrap the poor birds in puff pastry
and boil, or was it broil
one and one-half hours.
If boil, did those bundles of flaky dough
and meat rise to the top like thoughts
that agitate an easy answer to the thing?
Rolling out the dough,
keeping it wrapped tight around their folded wings,
not to forget the sage.
Cruel neighbors did cruel things:
beat an owl with a stick
goaded the whipped bull with dogs.
Could you believe them on the street?
And the opossum; nothing's plain and easy,
grub-sized progeny
traversing the saliva-slicked trail
to the envelope pouch.

WINTERING, WITNESS

They hunker down, stare, search, feed,
they are dark lines of type across winter sky,
solitary in bare branches along the highway
heat under feathers and down, eyes staring into dried grass
for the shake of a meadow vole or shrew,
a speck on rough bark, stilled.

They perch on the carcass in the puddled, brown field.
They land below the feeder, wings outspread over talons.
Brains shifting,
they flock before a storm to eat plentifully
of the seed at the feeder.

They take their serrated bills down below the floating ice
to come up with the muscle-flanked fish,
heat-makers, resilient.

They stand in the water, ice slivering around legs,
they keep their form, they keep their warmth,
white cheek feathers, black heads,
they are breasting the choppy waves off the rocks,
massed beyond the surf in flocks.

*

The beached boat: White Haven
on its transom and name of the town
across the bay it came from, sand in the cockpit
and sloping along the two bunks
in the galley, a bleached beer can and clumps
of rockweed, combings split.
The wrecks off the town pier in fog: rusty spikes.
The girl in the photo—
how small she was below those frames.
Rage against the falling apart,
the fever, the timbers blackening in sand.

*

They fly up from barnacled rocks as waves crash
they land, bills probing, fly up,
they flock on the lawn of the picturesque lighthouse
a few white feathers left behind
turn all in one direction.
Off the beach they float, pull heads back,
flip-tops, jostle and display.
They initiate courtship now, January, the cold salt bay
and long flight. They fly, silhouetted
against weathered backdrops,
the boarded-up houses.

MIGRANT: *PHILOHELA MINOR*

In a run of normal years that great eccentric Time, begets other years, different,
prodigal years, which—like a sixth, smallest toe—grow a thirteenth freak month.

—Bruno Schulz

First the maples, yellow, then browns, grays, mill town I skirted in snow.
Slushy roads, houses pushed up against the hillside. Water ice-edged, then
blue, people fishing along the dam. I drove into rain, into the fringe of
green in woods, a horse rolled in a paddock.

Someone's lawn ornaments were heads and tails of porpoises surfacing, hind
end of a plastic beagle pointed skyward—someone must have thought: let's
stick the beagle butt here in the daffodils. No one ever sat on the deck of
the one restaurant above water, its neon sign: Narragansett.

Bruno Schulz, your dull students survived the war, some orphaned, some
not. Here is a story: In Holland, a man makes bellows of plastic milk jugs,
air pumping and filling the lungs. Legs, ribs, limbs of white pvc, he trans-
ports them to the beach. Released, the Strandbeests circle and articulate—
Eiffel Towers, stilt creatures, they lurch and stride into the sea wind, past
the wagging dogs, scarf-bound walkers.

I drive to work and drive home through the mill town. Every spring, *Philo-*
hela minor—"bog lovers," the woodcocks twitter and fill the sky at dusk. A
bird your condor father would have loved, would have arranged weddings
for in his aviary under the stairs. Graham-cracker-and-soot patterned, part
of the leaf-litter, part of the sky.

Prodigal, how many birds lost from their wintering grounds, scent of wild
plum and sphagnum. In the rose-papered parlor, your father assumes the
shape of an emaciated condor. Marla's folding shapes of birds out of dark
paper, her gift to us. They swoop from the upstairs window, join the bats in
their wobbling flight.

DON'T TELL ME

it's iron, the bottle
crouched on its white pedestal,
long beak spout and wide open handle
you could see starry sky through.

Everybody was doing that new stitch,
it had spread far West, oh yes,
said Mrs. _____ at Knit & Purl,
but how many hats can one person wear?

I'd like to be more useful—say
apprentice to a bung fitter, or make
chipped ice, to hit something (not live)
on the head, directly,

I've not yet seen the Rock Wren
though I saw a photo of one inserting
pebbles in the airflow pipe of a mine,
therein to lay its eggs.

ENTOMOLOGY

Whereas before   it didn't matter
you became an odd thing
hating the story where the skull's dragged,
the boy who can't read,

fox bark over the hill
by the river and swamp maples,
the one road over the one bridge
unless it swims.

Come the season of cutworms,
light expanded—
bolts of striped awning
to cover the chair's bare sticks,
    roar of robins
in the yard where the rhubarb
spread its shade, eye fixed
on a bee,

this became our story. Stop
patching things together,
your mother put her tragic lens
to the world,
moth-wing dust in a glass
of drinking water.

An hour   two hours
a full day the dragonfly pulled
from its crackly nymph case—

No discernible movement
more of its milky-green body
out of the brown husk,

split down the back. Legs eased out
wing and wing   a day later
it could have spanned
your wrist, wings sheer as Saran wrap

the blank-eyed,
alien skin-shed hanging,
one leg fastened.

CALENDAR

All dark, compost-dirt rich, the mink
ran over the snow, brown muzzle
leading its body to rodent holes.
It slid into the river, neat as an exhale
under the pock-marked ice,
then out, dry-furred along the rocks.
Far out on the hill, someone skiing
broke a new trail in snow, called out:
just one more run, just one. Yellow tree light,
three-thirty, half the hill already dark.
Potatoes wrapped in foil soften in coals,
orange spheres, split, in the house
where we thought no one lived, a curtain
shifts, someone checking where the light was now.

THE ENCYCLOPEDIA OF MOTHS

Moths called owlets, a moth called sphinx. I looked for the name of the moth, form it should have taken in the garden: dark pupa, or caterpillar—notes filled index cards, lines, a paragraph, pages becoming longer until the red-bellied woodpecker hiding seeds in bark entered, the nicotiana calyx and its spill of seeds.

I simply could not see how to get from here to where they were steam-bending frames for the boat deep in the woods.

The reservoir was covered in snow, a few dark islands, pines, I saw myself in an inflatable suit, waterproof, buoyant, that pulled me up again and again on my skis from the growing puddles of water and slush. I thought it hilarious: all-purpose suit buoying me over the melting and refreezing surface.

Moths gathered on the yellow shingles of the house in winter. Rhododendrons, leaves curled to cigarettes, drooped in the cold. Small, dusky brown, like folded-over page corners meant to be reread, fifty, a hundred moths stippled the wall, dropped like stones to the step when touched.

The Cecropia, half its unfolding fits on plate VIII, Strawberry leaf-roller, Misnamed Gall-moth, the one that plumbs the heart of false indigo, swells the stem to a lumpen shelter, larvae "hidden in a few seared and silk-strewn leaves," the glass-green Gooseberry Fruit-worm that empties berries and fastens a cluster with a web of silk.

In the spent garden, a fluorescent green caterpillar among dry twigs and snags, the brown nicotiana's split seedpods that spilled a whoosh of seeds in November. Hairless, soft-skinned caterpillar, with a carmine horn, the next cold morning it's a brown twist on the sage, unrecognizable, out of season.

It should have dug in, dug down, formed a pupa there in a dirt hollow ("shaped like a hen's egg") waiting spring, waiting a gardener to dig it up.

In diapause, in metamorphosis, the pupa waits, its body turned to mush, moth-seed, moth-pod, like a storm cloud, like trees in winter. The light over the reservoir was the color of moth wings on glass, painted. The sky's winter-tinge, flat above the snow that had fallen on the reservoir and road I followed, to where they were shaping frames to fit snug in the hull; the boat that would be eased out of the woods, and into the water, eventually.

GLAZE

White putty under finger nails,
milky on fingerprints and the back of your t-shirt,
pushed between mullion and glass
it curls away when I press
and pull back my hand, putting the glass in,
to glaze.

A pane in the bedroom
fallen onto the porch, three jagged
pieces and a handful of splinters
on grainy shingles. Sash too soaked
to set the new glass.
                                Outside in the dark,
sloppy wet lilacs. The dog restless,
cold pressing at the curtain of yellow in cloth
I sewed, too yellow, it suffuses the room.
One window with a pie-piece, broken corner
the squirrel stuck its head through
before it leaped to the apple's trunk,

the road, gallery with its paintings,
landscapes and glazed pots.
To not keep it at bay: the glaze of frost on shingles,
grass blades tipped in minty relief,
the infinite angles of trunk and leaf
and the white lilacs, Lincoln's coffin, the broken window
the wind comes through from that teeming world,
carrying the mosquitoes and salt.

THE GARDEN WHISPERER

Hush, you little bastard, grow. Swim out into
greenery. *The Language of Plants*—a book,
once a contraption set up on the folding table
in science class. Swim through leaves
of summer, passion flowers in terracotta pots,
hooks and blues, crooks of stamens. Smartweed's
red seedpearl blossoms point to the creek, jewel-
weed, candelabra primrose, a rabbit's pleasure
of grass and goldenrod. The vegetable plot
a press of kale's edges. In April we crept through on
hands and knees, scraped deep for the cutworms'
dirt-tinged bodies pulsing with the green of
leeks and lettuce, beans snipped clean from the dirt.
The hummingbird's wing-beat tossed coral bells.
Give them what they want: water, dirt friable,
scratched free of stone and weed nodes,
iron shavings left from the farrier.

Goosefoot and chickweed. Who cares anymore? Picked
a bulbous squash from the seedy compost heap.
Cicada's grind of midday. The cabbage moth's
larvae snuggle up on the plants' ribs. Blake the cat,
watching from a stone wall. Monarchs, black zebras
wander from flower to flower of the weeds let go.

GLACIAL ERRATIC

Henry Moore's sheep
became the field edge and shade drift,
became the hillsheep across from the P. O.
where I lick my stamps,
thunder line at dusk spreading over
the darkened sound, the slick hull
                safely arrived
all loose ends fastened down.
Became their shapes, bleats, teats,
their feeding and steady gaze
into the studio windows
where he worked,
            field-bound.
Became the melons on straw,
became Bishop Snope saying, love wastefully.

The chipmunk took the green apples,
it ate gooseberries, too,
and the sunflower seeds planted in rows,

all summer it hoarded and fed.
The sheep became their easy arrangements,
their shorn selves, their thesaurus.
Became beans swelling in pods,
curled beak of the cotyledon
inside the green light.
Here the strange forehead of the other
                and stark joy.
Became sheep, their bolstered selves,
the ground and bedrock field.

CHRYSANTHEMUMS

You worked on the frame
of one window a whole day,
then another, sow bugs

in soft handfuls, a wool blanket
and desiccated mouse
found between walls—

long legs drawn up, shroud
of wool, like a miniature
squirrel ready to spring

to branch or eave.
The barn scrunched in
closer to the house at night,
last year's stories
beaten to thin bottle caps,
crumbled dirt.

The white cat with the broken tail
patrolled the yard,
brother to the one

that disappeared.
Beyond the window frame,
the river lifted scarlet leaves, rain

blackened trunks, we were here
last year. At work
unsold chrysanthemums

got tossed. Below zero nights
sprinklers kept on
to keep the buds from freezing,
the whole field of ice

in the sun, melting and shattering
the heaped ice cracklings
of rayed blooms.

SOMEWHERE IN SPACE

[Calico gray, rag-tag she chose our crawl space]

Calico gray, rag-tag she chose our crawl space,
pile of insulation unmoored to the floor
or ceiling, entry above the plywood
tacked there, temporary cover for the hole
beneath the house. Dark body circled,
eyes panned back at the flashlight,
miner's glint.
She chose the dark cave under the shed
in summer, trail of kittens
out to the thick iris fronds' swaying shelter,
the runt, ripple of white and gray,
calico, orange kitten who bent his shape
growling, over the heart of a chipmunk.

*

[They know their terrain, their paths]

They know their terrain, their paths,
materialize for food, for sun
slip into the broken panel of the coldframe
to sleep on the lettuce and beet shoots,
wary, they eye the trap, cornered
twist and dash, eddy of tight muscles,
eyes dilate. What am I, setting traps?—
someone hates them, someone tolerates them
someone wants to tame them.
Their route through the back field
of chickory and goldfinches, woodpile
to porch steps and the prickly gooseberry
where they rub their faces.
Over the back wall and gone,
feral orbits scrutinized.
They can't be relocated they know
the wren in its frenzy on the fence,
dog who does not chase.

*

["On foot"]

"On foot
I had to walk through the solar systems,
before I found the first thread of my red dress"

Edith Södergran
cradles her huge cat Totti in the photos
on the borders of her country, the critics

hate her poems, she and her mother
in the Russian dacha in the Finnish town

where she speaks German writes in Swedish,
food supplies cut off, TB,

the townspeople think she's mad.
Totti in sun, Totti on a chaise lounge

electric fur, paws curled,
the Russians shoot her cat, his

remarkable face-spots, blissed-out gaze
in her arms in all the photos except the first

studio portrait: a child in a plaid dress,
stuffed chaffinch on her arm, wings

spread to the left and right margins.

*

[In a week they are gone, did the mother]

In a week they are gone, did the mother
give a special call to signal we are moving
follow me, did the black snake come,
scream of the fisher, its minky body,
was it dusk, at dark. Stillness enfolds the yard
and garden, land the child knows
where raspberries grow in the garden,
wild blackberries, where the fox grapes
dropped to the pine needles.
If you ask (dim adult): How did you remember? . . .
silence, the cats' dark tunnel under the shed
empty now. Even the grandmother's song
of the cat coming back won't
return them now, further afield: path
by the river, old quarry where laurels
bloom, right angle turn along the fence.

*

[After I dumped the failed jelly by the rotten]

After I dumped the failed jelly by the rotten
herring I felt better

some things you cannot save, and they were
feral, the cats who appeared over the wall, like smoke
slid into the underbrush of dark jewelweed

and viburnums by the stream, though I tried
to watch their night movements,
tried to know their lives,

one solitary in snow, footprints
over the woodpile, under the back steps
down the path to the chicken coop.

One, clown-like Ripple on the grape arbor
chased dry leaves, wind tracing the yard,

        and didn't the orioles wing down
to eat the jelly, and some night wanderer
leave a neat hole
where the herring was buried.

*

[If you count the catalogue of cats]

If you count the catalogue of cats
famished cats, cats in the woodpile, dawn barn cats
catching the milk stream, cats in the kitchen,
ember of cat spoor in snow,
wartime cats, war babies sent to another country
(how do you say cat how do you say milk)
cats in the belfry, are you crazy says my mother
no one had vets for cats those days, crazy rooms
of women and cats, cats at the farm,
cats in the river, cats in a sack.
                              Because
they are feral they don't want
our pats or cuddles, not the cats of childhood,
cats that we fed that moved in and out
of the house, lounged on windowsills, cat
that slept on my head at night so I dozed
in fear of her claws and called muffled
my parents in the far reaches of the house.

                    *

[A lens of cloud, a sighting around a sheet]

A lens of cloud, a sighting around a sheet
of white, what can she see, the cat
with the injured eye. Thorn bush, rat bite,
I follow her through grass, her path to the tractor
seat warmed by sun, her eye a swirled cloud,
white marble. A week in spring and it does not
get better. I borrow traps, open tuna
and now she stays further away. In Virginia
my aunt is ill, who with her own
failed sight could lob back a tennis ball
faster than I could run to it, who was in
San Francisco when the Pacific fleet returned
under the Golden Gate Bridge, said they threw
their caps in the air and everybody cheered
that generation, what will we do. Lights reflect
on the Thames River, New London skyline,
what will we see?

*

[Coming back into the yard something's off]

Coming back into the yard something's off—
a spot: white and orange hovers
against the green, moves, floats,

jags back and forth against the brush line—
it's a swan, blundered into the back yard

sway and careen it jabs and jabs
head through the fence, against the closed gate,

over the ditch, list and jab it can't
fly up, I open the gate, shush-shush
it through, careening it knows exactly where

in the world it wants to go,
straight into woods, heaves itself over

briars and logs, disappearing white spot in the dense
brush on short legs fast, unsteady-seeming,

direction of the river, it goes.

*

[She is back, the one-eyed cat, trapped]

She is back, the one-eyed cat, trapped
vetted, released, denizen of the woodpile
and crawl space, garden beds warm from sun. Attrition
of fall the garden thins out, a few cats
return to snooze in the chives, under the apple.
Some have disappeared though I call
and call and watch at dusk.
The child says: "I buried a beetle yesterday"
on how long a dragonfly lives; me: "a day."
Child: "No! a year."
"How do you know, well, some insects only live
a day . . ." but in the book of dragon and damsel flies,
sure enough: a year.
A feral cat lives 1 to 3 years, a house cat
more than 12. In my dream a dark-furred cat
appears, arching its back
sore-covered, surprisingly tame.

*

[Edith Södergran, also holding the leash]

Edith Södergran, also holding the leash
of a Karelian bear dog ("a hunter
of unyielding bravery and determination")
wrote

"somewhere in space hangs my heart" and
"sparks fly from it, shaking the air."

Yesterday I thought: I want a birch tree,
there, and saw three slim trunks in a clump, my only
deliberate thought: three white lines

vertical and the cats weaving in and around them
and the girl on the rock under the birches.

If a cat nests under your shed
is it your work to nudge and cajole
the offspring into domesticity,

if a wren nests in your yard, surely you will give it
a wide berth until the nestlings fledge. Planetary

your movements around them—
their incendiary hearts.

TOWN RUNWAY

Runway lights, precise points
like the blue eyes of scallops.
At the edge, deer in fog, the herd feeding,
necks reach heads up and sidereal ears
open to any wave of sound.
A father bundles his not-sleepy-enough child,
walks to the woods' edge,
burdock, goldenrod, and pokeweeds'
wide leaves and heavy, wine-dark berries.
On the runway, the lights' steady blinking,
sumac turning flame in fall,
dusk coming sooner and in the predawn
the herd culled from the runway,
where they spent their days grazing
below the huge shapes, loud,
that passed over them, that blocked light
and came in closer at the same intervals
every day, between the white gulls
dropping clams on the tarmac.
At the boat, Carl from the restaurant
came to the foot of the ladder
and offered hot stew: broth,
vegetables, venison from the culled herd
because you were working late.
A huge squash, head-sized,
grew up between tarmac and weeds,
damp with dew, strings of pulp and seeds
spilled from the split flesh.
I was cooking again, house warm
from the stove, at night, the owl
in the neighbor's yard. But he is no longer
our neighbor, but he was, is no longer,
it was still his yard, we believed
half a year not knowing he had died.
The owl calling from the tangle
of brush and cedars. All those months,
accepting a squash, a bowl of venison stew,
and a boat from the man who culled

the deer, thinking our neighbor was there
in the fog-bound field, the old yam farm,
arrowhead mound above the river.
The cookbook saying a bitter salad would go well
with squash bisque and apple comfit.

DAYS OF THE PHARAOH

A falcon eyes a dusty brown quail,
days of the rising Nile, silted fields
we tended, barley, bread rising
in clay jars, honey and grit.
23 years, your yearly procession
down the Nile to check on our progress:
weights of building blocks,
the carvings and causeways.
Before sun, ducks rose from the flooded
fields, goose with its grey eye patch
and trail of goslings. If you,
then us, too, why did no one
say that? Your boats prepared
in their stone pits, oars and sail,
blue amulets. Some of our men
left from the village and never
returned, their mallets and string lines saved.
Cats waited on white butterflies,
stared down iridescent beetles.
The river brought everything to the site,
rafts of goods, linen-bound ibis,
cattle, sheep, the slim dog
along for the ride, asleep on drying
papyrus. Pharaoh—
in your leaving you diminished us.
Even the small shrew in its heat,
its dash through reed stems
and light dappled bank,
had a net of haste about it,
little conduit, narrow blood artery
who am I to channel this,
snail's scrollwork written over.

APPLES

I kept my toads in a cage
circled beneath the apple tree.

They said I was cold, I was not
but I stole, see me there at dusk
thinking no one cared about the apples they were abandoned,
carrying them home, t-shirt heavy

bulging with their weight and roundness,
in the softening green, tree limbs glowing.

We go back to patterns, the circles
weeded beneath trees I repeat here, dirt
crumbled and heaped up neatly like a dry mix
before baking. Or, how laying out the garden plan,
I shaped out rectangles, beds jutting out

from the stone wall, anchored there
perpendicular-wise.
I merely watched was aware
of the toads' round-shouldered figures
coming out from the sage at night
their gold-flecked eyes. Remembering
one that long ago followed me into the house,

silent familiar in the corner
on the wood-floored porch, or by the garbage pail.

In a cage of twigs and chicken wire
below the orchard's trees. Go back
to the monk's tour of Manhattan Island's orchards

1715, "Stone Fruits in Sweete Abundance."
the caged toads at the bases of trees
unmolested by the dog who looks over them, inscrutable
as to their bitterness.

A sticky globe, apple red, tangles flies in the boughs,
the toads are rewarded:

the sweet taste of coddling moths
the steady plowing grubs that come to the trees.

There's always more to think of regarding apples:
the graft enclosed in wax-bound string,
a severed and healed branch.
Roots seeking calcium,
growing into the skeletons of Roger and Mary Williams.

This apple tree, floating in the back field,
but not really alone: the grubs, toads,
green smudge of lichen on its limbs,

the great crested flycatcher who shrieks above
later in the summer season
across the stone wall, another apple's buds,
the calcium in our bones
bearing our sweet weight into evening.

NOTES

"How It Sounds": "They have their own vocabulary . . ." is from *Bird Sounds and Their Meaning* by Rosemary Jellis (Cornell UP, 1977). "[W]aves of high-pitched sounds . . ." and "On bright winter days white-throated sparrows . . ." are from *Watching Birds* by Roger F. Pasquier (Houghton Mifflin, 1977).

"Two Gourds": "A belief in the night in which the corn grows" is from Henry David Thoreau.

"Baking Soda Trading Cards: Bird Series": The trading cards were released by Church & Dwight Co., Inc., sellers of Arm & Hammer and Cow Brand Baking Soda and found in the boxes of baking soda. Early artists were M. C. Eaton, G. Moss Arnholt, and Hy Hintermeister. In the early 1920s, the artist and ornithologist Louis Agassiz Fuertes supplied bird illustrations for the cards. Quotes are from the cherished, torn, and dog-eared cards, kept in a drawer for decades, with a split rubber band wrapped around the deck. "And no birds sang" is a reference to Rachel Carson's *Silent Spring*.

"History of Private Life": The title is inspired by reading a volume of *A History of Private Life*, the series published by Harvard University Press.

"Migrant: *Philohela minor*": The quote by Bruno Schulz is from the story "The Night of the Great Season" collected in *The Street of Crocodiles*, trans. Celina Wieniewska (Penguin, 1963). (The American Woodcock is now *Scolopax minor*; it's no longer called *Philohela minor*.)

"The Encyclopedia of Moths": "[S]haped like a hen's egg" is from Gene Stratton Porter's description of the hollow in the dirt around a pupa from *Moths of the Limberlost*. "[H]idden in a few seared and silk-strewn leaves" is from *The Moth Book: A Popular Guide to a Knowledge of the Moths of North America*, W. J. Holland (Doubleday, Page & Co., 1914).

"Somewhere in Space": Edith Södergran (1892–1923). Quotes from *Love & Solitude: Selected Poems 1916–1923*, trans. Stina Katchadourian (Fjord Press, 1981). During the war the children were bundled off to Sweden—the luggage-tagged children put on the train. My mother's family had cats, not many households did back then—cats were for the farms. At our house the feral cat had her kittens under the shed.

Blessings the Body Gave
WALT McDONALD

Anatomy, Errata
JUDITH HALL

Stones Don't Float: Poems Selected and New
JOHN HAAG

Crossing the Snow Bridge
FATIMA LIM-WILSON

The Creation
BRUCE BEASLEY

Night Thoughts and Henry Vaughan
DAVID YOUNG

History as a Second Language
DIONISIO D. MARTINEZ

Guests
TERESA CADER

Rooms, Which Were People
MARY CROSS

The Book of Winter
SUE OWEN

Life-list
ROBERT CORDING

Popular Culture
ALBERT GOLDBARTH

CPSIA information can be obtained
at www.ICGtesting.com
Printed in the USA
FFHW021553310719
53993672-59714FF